D1326381

Romans, Saxons & Vikings

Living in Anglo-Saxon England

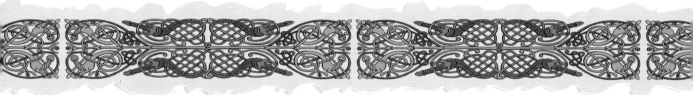

Martyn Whittock

First published in Great Britain by
Heinemann Library
Halley Court, Jordan Hill, Oxford OX2 8EJ
a division of Reed Educational & Professional
Publishing Ltd

MELBOURNE AUCKLAND
FLORENCE PRAGUE MADRID ATHENS
SINGAPORE TOKYO CHICAGO SAO PAULO
PORTSMOUTH NH MEXICO
IBADAN GABORONE JOHANNESBURG
KAMPALA NAIROBI

© Reed Educational & Professional
Publishing Ltd 1996

Designed by Ken Vail Graphic Design

Origination by Magnet Harlequin Group

Illustrations by Ken Vail Graphic Design

Printed in the UK by Jarrold Book Printing, Thetford

00 99 98 97 96

10 9 8 7 6 5 4 3 2 1

ISBN 0 431 05966 7

British Library Cataloguing in Publication Data

Whittock, Martyn J. (Martyn John)
Living in Anglo-Saxon England. – (Romans,
Saxons, Vikings)
1. Great Britain – History – Anglo-Saxon period,
449 – 1066 – Juvenile literature
2. Great Britain – Social life and customs – To 1066
– Juvenile literature
I. Title II. Series 941'.017

Acknowledgements

The Publishers would like to thank
the following for permission to
reproduce photographs.

British Museum: p.4, 8, 10, 17, 19, 24,
25, 26, 27; David Hinton: p.23;
Martyn Whittock: p.14; Michael
Holford: p.5; Michael Hughes: p.11;
National Museums of Scotland: p.8;
Norfolk Museums Service: p.5;
Ordnance Survey: p.6

Cover photograph reproduced with
permission of the British Library.

Our thanks to Keith Stringer, of the
Department of History at Lancaster
University, for his comments in the
preparation of this book.

We would like to thank the following
schools for valuable comments made
regarding the content and layout of
this series: Fitzmaurice Primary
School, Bradford-on-Avon, Wiltshire;
Tyersal School, Bradford, Yorkshire.

Details of written sources

M. Alexander (trans), *Earliest English
Poems*, Penguin 1977: 6B; 7A

C. Fell, *Women in Anglo-Saxon
England*, British Museum
Publications 1984: 13A

S. Keynes, M. Lapidge (trans), *Alfred
the Great*, Penguin 1983: 1B

L. Sherley-Paige (trans), *History of the
English Church and People*, Penguin
1968: 9A

**For Jessica Whittock, with love
from Uncle Martyn.**

Contents

Clues from the past

Different kinds of clues have survived from Anglo-Saxon times. We use these as evidence when deciding how people lived.

Anglo-Saxons ruled England from about AD450 (southeast only) until AD1066. They did not come to this country in one great invasion. They crossed the sea from Europe, in small groups, in the fifth and sixth centuries AD.

We can find out about them from different clues which have survived from this time. Some of these clues can be seen here. Some clues were lost in the past. Over time they became covered by dirt. Some clues were buried on purpose. Many are found by **archaeologists**. They dig up these things and study them.

Lost clues

Lots of clues have been lost, for many reasons.

- Wood often rots away.

- Gold and silver can be melted down and used again.

- Iron rusts away.

- Books were rare. Most people could not read or write. Some of these rare books have been lost or destroyed. We know more about what people made, like pots and houses, than about what they thought and felt.

Source A

*This is a **brooch** made of silver. It was made in about AD850. Only rich people wore brooches like this. We do not always know what poorer people wore.*

Source B

I, King Alfred, ordered to be written down the laws our fathers obeyed. These were the laws I agreed with. The ones I did not agree with I rejected.

The Anglo-Saxon King Alfred writing about how he ordered a book of laws to be written. He wrote this in about AD890. Most people could not write, so we do not know what they thought.

Source C

Some stone buildings survive from Anglo-Saxon times. This is the Church of St Laurence, in Bradford-on-Avon, Wiltshire. It was built in about AD1000. Most buildings, though, were made of wood, and they have not survived.

Source D

Digging up pots containing the remains of burnt bodies. These were found at Spong Hill, Norfolk. They date from about AD500. We do not know who the people buried here were. Cemeteries like this are often found by accident. In the past many were destroyed.

Anglo-Saxon place-names

Many names of modern places were first used in Anglo-Saxon times. They can tell us about life in those times.

The Anglo-Saxons made up different kinds of names for the places where they lived. These tell us things like:

- the person who owned the land;

- whether the place was a farm, a village or a town;

- which animals lived there;

- what the land was like;

- which crops grew there.

Source A

A map showing part of Wiltshire. The arrows show some of the place-names that are from Anglo-Saxon times. In the box to the right are the meanings of these names in Old English.

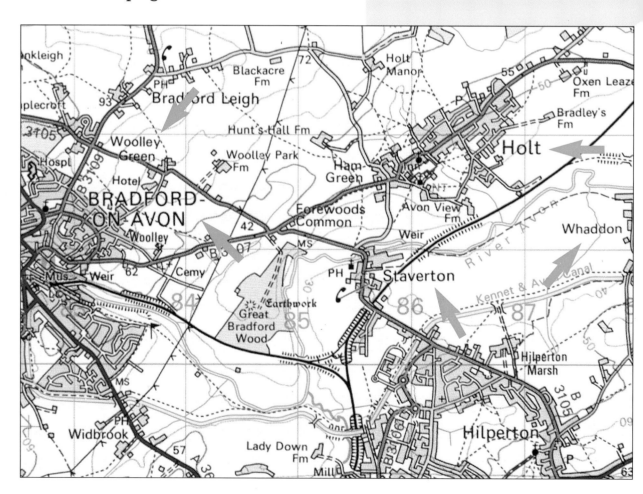

- Holt means 'a wood'.
- Staverton means 'the village by a pole'.
- Whaddon means 'hill where a plant called woad grows'.
- Woolley means 'clearing where there are wolves'.
- Bradford means 'the broad, or wide ford'.

How do we know?

Each of the place-names listed above has Anglo-Saxon words in it. By finding out the meaning of these words we can find out what each place-name means. These names can tell us things about life in the past. We can see that wolves lived near Woolley, for instance, and we can see which plants grew at Whaddon. This is not always easy. To do it, we need to know about the language of the Anglo-Saxons.

The Anglo-Saxons' language is called Old English. This is not the same as the language we speak today. It has changed over the past 1,000 years. Because of this, it is not always easy to understand what place-names mean.

Some Old English words and what they mean

These words can still be found in modern place-names. Do any places near you have these words in their names?

- **bury** fort, or a large town
- **burn** stream
- **cot** small house
- **combe** small valley
- **dun** hill
- **ford** a place where a river can be crossed
- **ham** village
- **holt** wood
- **ley** clearing in a wood
- **mere** lake
- **tun** another word for village
- **worth** farm

The Anglo-Saxon kingdoms

Anglo-Saxon England was split up into different kingdoms. These kingdoms changed as some got bigger by conquering others.

The Anglo-Saxons came to this country when the Romans stopped ruling Britain. Some came as **warriors**, to raid and steal. Others came to settle and find new homes. Some fought with the British people who lived here before the Anglo-Saxons arrived. Others mixed with the British peacefully and worked with them.

Where did the Anglo-Saxons first settle?

The first Anglo-Saxons arrived on the south and east coasts of Britain. They set up little kingdoms. These were Kent, Wessex, Sussex, Essex and East Anglia. Each of these little kingdoms had its own **king**.

The Anglo-Saxons conquer more land

After about AD550 some of these kingdoms began to grow. Anglo-Saxon kings and warriors conquered more land, and soon there were even more little kingdoms. Two of these later kingdoms were Mercia and Northumbria, but there were other, smaller kingdoms, as well.

Source A

*The type of **brooch** worn by a rich Anglo-Saxon. This one is from Yorkshire and was made in about AD850.*

Source B

The type of brooch worn by rich British people. This one is from Ayrshire, in Scotland, and was made in about AD700.

8

A country called England

The land that the Anglo-Saxons conquered came to be called England. This was because the Anglo-Saxons called themselves the 'Englisc'. This means 'English' in their language. England means 'Land of the English'. Eventually the kings of Wessex became rulers of all England.

The British people

The Anglo-Saxons did not take control of Wales and Scotland. In the west and north of England there were fewer Anglo-Saxon settlers. Here, British people did not always dress and speak like the Anglo-Saxons living in other parts of England. Some carried on living as they had done before the Anglo-Saxons arrived.

Northumbria

Mercia

East Anglia

Essex

Wessex

Kent

Sussex

The most important Anglo-Saxon kingdoms by about AD650.

Farms and farmers

Most Anglo-Saxons lived in the country in small settlements. Poorer people lived in small houses.

Most people in Anglo-Saxon England were farmers who grew crops and kept animals. Most people would have lived all their lives and then died in the same part of the country. They did not travel much – and they did not live as long as people do today.

From farms to villages

The earliest Anglo-Saxons lived in small groups of farms. We call these small **settlements** 'hamlets'. The farms and other buildings in the hamlets were pulled down and rebuilt every few years. This was because they were made of wood and thatch, which rotted and needed to be replaced. This meant that the settlement was often changing.

In time, many of these little settlements grew into villages. These were larger, more organized and better planned. Many eventually had a little Christian church, too. These were first built of wood and later of stone.

Source A

All that remains of a type of house lived in by poorer people. All the wood and thatch has rotted away. All that is left is the hole in the ground.

Source B

Pieces of baked clay used to hold down the threads when weaving cloth. These were found on the floor of an Anglo-Saxon house at Sutton Courtenay, in Berkshire.

Houses in the countryside

Archaeologists have discovered some Anglo-Saxon villages. There were often lots of little buildings scattered about. Many had floors dug below the level of the ground. They probably had thatched roofs held up by wooden poles, and would probably have looked like tents. They were lived in by the poorest people.

Some of these houses probably had wooden floors. The space underneath might have been used to store things. It might have helped keep the house warm and dry. Some of these buildings were used as workshops. **Craftworkers** used them as places to make **pottery**, or to weave wool into cloth.

The smaller houses were often grouped around a larger building. This was the **hall**, where the richer people lived. The biggest halls were lived in by **lords** who owned a lot of land.

How do we know?

The remains of the house (Source A) show us that it had a floor dug into the ground. Dark patches in the soil show where there were wooden posts. This shows that the house had a roof. Pieces of rotten wood show us that it had walls made from wooden planks.

Source B shows that people often worked in houses like this.

Different kinds of people in the village

There were different groups of people living in the villages. Rich and poor people were treated differently.

Some people in the countryside were rich **lords**. They owned a lot of land, which was given to them by the king. These lords were called 'thegns' (pronounced 'thanes'), in the language of the Anglo-Saxons. Below them were people called freemen, or 'ceorls' (pronounced 'churls'). These people owned a smaller amount of land. They had to serve in the army if the king told them to, and they sometimes had to work on the lord's land without any pay. Some poorer freemen had very little land. They had to do a lot of work for their lord. There were also priests, who led Christian worship. They were often given land by the lords and food by the village people.

Slaves

The hardest work was done by **slaves**. They were not free. They were owned by their lords. Some had been made slaves because they had broken the law. Some had been captured in wars. Some had become so poor that they sold themselves to a lord. The lord then gave them food. Children of slaves had to be slaves, too.

Source B

Anglo-Saxon farmers harvesting and ploughing. The picture at the bottom shows the lord resting and drinking with his followers. These pictures were painted in about AD1030.

How do we know?

The pictures (Source B) show us that life was different for rich and poor people. The ordinary people are working hard in the fields. The rich lords are eating and drinking inside.

The laws (Source A) also show that rich people were treated differently from poorer people. Anglo-Saxons thought that the life of a lord was worth more than the life of a poorer person. But richer people did have to pay more money than poor people if they let the king down.

Bloodprice

The Anglo-Saxons believed that if a person hurt or killed someone else they had to pay money to show they were sorry. This was called paying 'wergeld', or 'bloodprice.' A small amount was paid if a person was slightly injured. More was paid if the person was badly injured or killed. More money had to be paid if the person who had been hurt was a lord, than if he was a freeman. This was because the lords were thought to be more important.

Living in the lord's hall

Rich people lived in large wooden houses called halls.

Anglo-Saxon **lords** lived in larger houses than their poorer neighbours. These houses were called **halls**. They had high roofs held up by wooden posts and walls made from planks. The hall usually had two large doors facing each other. Building a hall took a lot of skill and time. Many people were needed to build it.

What did a hall look like?

The roof might have been thatched, or some halls might have had roofs made of wooden tiles. The walls and doors may have been carved and painted.

Later halls may have had an upstairs, too. This would have left space underneath, and food and drink could be kept there.

Living in the hall

The lord and his followers lived in the hall. The followers were the lord's **warriors** and his most important servants. The hall was where they all ate and met together. At night everyone slept in the hall – there were no private bedrooms. There were no bathrooms or toilets in the hall, either.

How do we know?

Source B tells us that halls needed a lot of people to build them, and it tells us that they had tall roofs. Over the years these halls have rotted away. All that is left are rows of dark marks in the dirt. These are where the posts stood in the ground. Because of this we do not know what the roofs were like.

Source A shows that later halls had rooms upstairs. This was where the lord met his followers. Underneath was space to store things.

We have to be careful, though. Source B is a poem. The poet may have made the hall sound grand to impress people. The person who made Source A might not have seen Harold's hall. The picture might show it with an upstairs just to make it look important.

Relaxing at home – games and riddles

We know that many rich and poor Anglo-Saxons enjoyed playing games and listening to simple poems and riddles.

Some early Anglo-Saxon bodies were buried with things used to play board games. In one cemetery, at Caistor near Norwich (in Norfolk), there were counters made from ivory and bone. These were found in one grave. In another grave 31 sheep bones were found. They had been used to play a game like **'jacks'**. Other bone playing-pieces have been found in graves from other parts of England.

Some people cheated at these games. Two dice were found in Norfolk which had been made so that they would always come up with a six!

Poems and riddles

Many people liked poems. They enjoyed simple poems about everyday life. They also liked to tell riddles. A riddle is a kind of poem. It describes something well known, but in a complicated or difficult way. You have to guess what it is about.

Source A

Frost shall freeze,
Fire eat wood,
Earth will grow,
Ice bridge water.

This poem about nature comes from a collection of Anglo-Saxon writings called the Exeter Book.

Source B

Over the waves I saw a strange thing,
Well made and wonderfully decorated:
A wonder on the waves – water become like bone.

An Anglo-Saxon riddle. What is it? The answer is 'ice'.

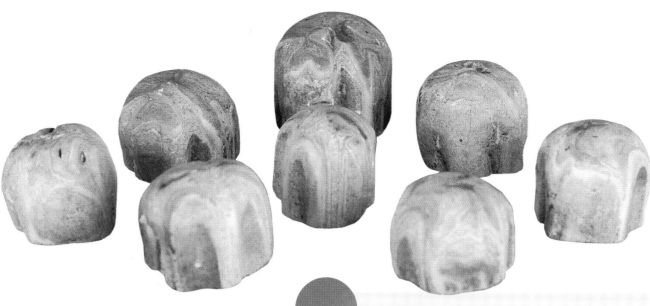

These counters were probably used to play a game. They are made from polished horses' teeth. They date from the seventh century and were found at Faversham, in Kent.

How do we know?

Source A shows a simple poem that people enjoyed. Source B shows that people made up riddles, too. Simple poems and riddles were about things used, or seen, in everyday life.

The pieces in Source C are probably from a game. They are carefully made. They look like counters, but we cannot be sure that they are from a game. If it was a game, we still do not know how it was played.

Eating and drinking

Poorer Anglo-Saxons could not afford the expensive wine enjoyed by rich **lords**. They would have drunk mead and beer. People often got drunk when relaxing. Sometimes eating and drinking ended in fights. At times people were hurt, or killed.

Relaxing at home – storytelling

Anglo-Saxon lords and their followers often relaxed by listening to stories.

Anglo-Saxon **lords** and their followers were brave **warriors**. They loved to hear stories about other brave warriors. At night the lord and his followers ate together in the lord's **hall**. As they ate and drank they often listened to stories. The lord's wife brought food and drink to the men. Other women helped her.

The storytellers

The people who told the stories often played music while they talked. They played **harps**, or lyres, which are like harps. The storytellers could not read or write. They listened to other people's songs and stories, then remembered them. Sometimes they made up their own stories. If the story was good the lord gave the storyteller presents like gold rings and **brooches**.

The warriors ate and drank while the storyteller was singing. When he finished, the warriors sometimes boasted. They boasted that they were brave, like the people in the stories. They promised they would fight for their lord.

Source A

It was a terrible battle. The warriors did not run away. They fought till they were hurt. Then they fell down dead. All the time Eadwald and his brother Oswald called to their friends to keep on fighting. All the time they swung their swords.

Part of an Anglo-Saxon story called 'The Battle of Maldon', written in the eleventh century. It was the kind of story warriors liked. It made them sound very brave.

Source B

A picture painted by an Anglo-Saxon artist, around the year AD750. It shows a person from the Bible, named King David, who was famous for writing songs. King David lived hundreds of years before the Anglo-Saxons. He was not an Anglo-Saxon but the artist made him look like one. The artist drew him playing a lyre, like an Anglo-Saxon storyteller.

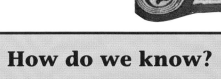

How do we know?

Source B shows that Anglo-Saxon storytellers played lyres as they told their stories. We can use this picture to tell how big these lyres were. It also shows how storytellers played them.

We cannot be sure that King David really played a lyre like this one. This picture is an Anglo-Saxon's idea of what he might have played. Anglo-Saxon artists often copied other pictures. We do not know when this picture was drawn for the very first time.

Towns and trade

Towns were in ruins when the Anglo-Saxons arrived. They later grew again, as trading places.

When the first Anglo-Saxons settled in this country, they found that the Roman towns were in ruins. This was because of the problems in Britain at the end of the Roman Empire. Only a few people were still living in towns.

Kings' halls in old Roman towns

Anglo-Saxon **kings** sometimes set up their **halls** in a crumbling Roman town. Perhaps they did this because they thought these had been special places. It was from these places that the Romans had run the country. The first Christian churches were often built in these ruined towns, too, near the halls of the kings and their followers.

Towns start to grow again

Very slowly, towns began to grow again. They were useful places, where people could buy and sell things. This is called **trade**. Kings could use the towns as places to sell animals and food from their own lands. They could buy expensive jewellery and goods from other countries.

Source A

The capital of the East Saxons is the city of London. It stands on the banks of the River Thames and is a trading centre for many nations. They come to it by land and sea.

Written by Bede, an Anglo-Saxon monk from Northumbria, in about AD731.

Source B

A piece of pottery from the early Anglo-Saxon town of Hamwic. This pottery was made in about AD800, in the Eifel mountains, in modern Germany. It would have been brought to Hamwic by a merchant.

How do we know?

Source B shows us that merchants travelled a long way to reach the market in the town of Hamwic. The Eifel mountains are over 400 miles from Hamwic. Merchants would only have come this far if they thought it was worth it. They must have wanted the things that were for sale at Hamwic. This shows that important trading was going on there. Source A shows that this was true of other trading towns, too.

Merchants from other countries

Goods would be brought to the markets in the towns by **merchants**. Kings could make sure that only their loyal followers were allowed to get hold of these things. This made these people like the king even more!

Early towns in England

One early town in Wessex was called Hamwic. It was where the town of Southampton is now. It had been set up by about AD710. Large numbers of cattle were brought here and exchanged for glass, wine, gold and silver from abroad.

Another early town, in northern England, was Eoforwic. It was where York is now. Another was at Lundenwic, west of Roman London.

Towns become more important

Over time, towns grew larger. They played an important part in Anglo-Saxon England.

Many different things were bought and sold. The Anglo-Saxons sold **slaves**, animal skins and leather. They bought things from overseas. Millstones, for grinding corn into flour, came from what is now Germany. **Pottery** and wine came from northern France and Belgium. Bronze bowls came from Egypt.

Trade from far away

Precious stones came from even further away. Red garnets came from India and Ceylon. Blue amethysts came from the Middle East. Cowrie shells came from the Red Sea. These had probably been bought and sold many times before they reached England.

The growing importance of towns

When the **Vikings** attacked England, the **kings** of Wessex built defences around their towns. These were called 'burhs'. This shows how important and rich these towns had become.

Source A

An Anglo-Saxon penny made in about AD1056. The writing on it says that it was made in the town of York. Coins had to say where they had been made. All coins had to be made in a town.

Source B

The earth wall around the town of Wareham, Dorset. This was in the kingdom of Wessex. The wall was built to defend the town from Viking attacks after AD878.

How do we know?

Source B shows how important towns had become. They were worth defending and capturing. Source A shows that the later Anglo-Saxon kings decided all coins had to be made in towns. Coins had to show the name of the town in which they were made.

Trade in towns

Later Anglo-Saxon kings made sure all trade took place in a town. They took money from the **merchants** who visited. Servants of the king checked that the buying and selling was done properly. They also made sure that coins were made in towns. The name of the town was put on each of the coins.

Towns at the end of Anglo-Saxon England

By AD1066 there were many towns in England. About one in ten people lived in a town. But towns were still much smaller than today. About 7,000 people lived in Norwich and 5,500 lived in Winchester. Many things were made, as well as sold, in towns. Pottery and goods made of bone and leather were made in towns. There were many Christian churches in towns. These were very important in the lives of the people.

Craftworkers – making things for everyday life

Many things used in everyday life were made by craftworkers.

Many Anglo-Saxons were skilled at making things. **Craftworkers** made things for a living. Mostly they made things out of metal and wood, or were skilled in weaving cloth. Some worked in villages, but over time more worked in the towns.

Carpenters

One skill was carpentry, which means making things out of wood. Carpenters made buckets and barrels, bowls and plates. Some carpenters built the great **halls** that the **lords** lived in. Others made ploughs and boats.

Source A

Part of a box made from carved ivory in about AD700. It shows a blacksmith at work. This blacksmith was not a real man but an Anglo-Saxon god, called 'Weland the Smith'.

A modern reproduction of a great iron chain used to hold a cooking pot over a fire, and found in an Anglo-Saxon **king's** grave at Sutton Hoo, in Suffolk. It was made in about AD620.

How do we know?

We can use Source A to tell us that Anglo-Saxon blacksmiths used tongs to hold hot pieces of metal. It also shows us that they hammered the hot metal on blocks of metal or stone called anvils. The fact that the Anglo-Saxons believed that one of their gods was a blacksmith shows that they thought this was a very important job.

Source B shows us a chain which held a cooking pot over a fire. It was so well made that it was buried with a king.

Blacksmiths

Craftworkers who made objects out of iron were blacksmiths. They used great hammers to hammer hot iron into different shapes. They hammered the iron on blocks of metal or stone called anvils.

Things made from metal

Blacksmiths made things like tools, nails and horseshoes. They made chains to hold cooking pots over fires. Other people made plates and jugs out of metals called pewter and lead.

Making cloth

In most towns and villages, wool was woven to make clothes. We know that many sheep were kept to produce the wool that was needed. A lot of this weaving would have been done by women.

Other skills

Other craftworkers made **pottery** out of clay. Others made soap and salt, or made charcoal from burnt wood. Blacksmiths used this as fuel to heat iron.

Making beautiful objects

Some craftworkers made rare and expensive objects.

Some Anglo-Saxon **craftworkers** made expensive things for rich people. They often made them for **kings**, **lords** and for churches.

Anglo-Saxon jewellery

Brooches were made from gold and silver. A red stone called garnet was often used. Many brooches were covered with patterns. These often showed the bodies of snakes and dragons mixed together.

Glassmaking

When the Romans left Britain, people forgot how to make glass. After AD600, people began to make it again. They started this at Faversham, in Kent. Some glass was made at the **monastery** of Monkwearmouth, in Northumbria. This glass was for windows and was very expensive. Over time, it became a little more common. Even so, only rich people could afford it.

Source A

Shoulder clasp jewellery, made in about AD620. It was found at Sutton Hoo, in Suffolk. It held up a cloak.

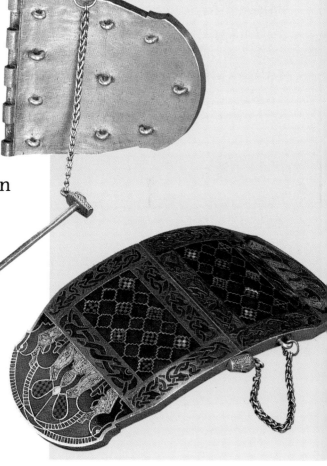

A page from a copy of the Bible. It comes from a monastery at Lindisfarne, in Northumbria. It was made in about AD698.

How do we know?

The jewellery and book show Anglo-Saxon skills. The jewellery needed skills in working with gold, glass and precious stones. The book pattern was drawn with a compass and ruler.

Sources A and B show how Anglo-Saxons liked to decorate beautiful objects. Both the jewellery and the book use the bodies of snakes, birds and dragons mixed together.

Illuminated books

Most people could not read or write. Books were all written by hand, and they were rare and expensive. They were carefully decorated. Books like this are called 'illuminated'. Many of these books were copies of the Bible. Some were books of prayers.

Women in Anglo-Saxon England

All Anglo-Saxon women were less independent than women today. They had less freedom, but some women owned land. These richer women could often read and were powerful people.

When a woman got married, her husband gave her a present. This was called a 'Morning Gift'. For rich people this was money and land. A woman could use this in any way she wished. Poorer women would be given a brooch, or pots.

Rich women owned large amounts of land. They got some land when their fathers died. Some land was given to them by their husbands. These women were important and powerful. Ethelfled, daughter of King Alfred, was one of the most powerful people in England. She was called 'The Lady of the Mercians'.

Marriage and family

Most marriages were arranged by the families of the people getting married. A woman had the right to refuse to marry a man she did not like. Women had the right to leave their husbands. They could sometimes take their children with them. If their husbands died, women could keep their children to look after them.

Source A

Leofgyth owns Knook. Her husband owned it before 1066. Leofgyth made and makes gold-thread **embroidery** for the **king** and queen.

*This evidence is from the **Domesday Book**. It tells how a woman named Leofgyth owned land. The land was in Wiltshire.*

Source B

If a man dies, leaving a wife and child, it is right that the child should stay with the mother. One of the husband's family should look after the property until the child is ten years old.

A law from Kent. It dates from the seventh century.

Source C

A picture showing Queen Elfgifu being given a book. It comes from about AD1025.

How do we know?

Source A shows that women could own land. It also shows that women sometimes worked at making cloth. As this was a rich woman, the work might have been done by her servants.

Source B shows that women could keep their children when their husbands died. But it also shows that they were not free to use their husband's money and land. This belonged to their children.

Source C shows that very rich women could read. This book was written especially for this queen.

Jobs done by women

Women were often responsible for making cloth. Poorer women made cloth for their families. Richer women may have made more expensive kinds of cloth. Often richer women had servants to make it for them.

In poorer families, women would have worked in the fields with their husbands. These women also ran the home and made sure the family was fed and clothed.

Glossary

archaeologists people who dig up and study things made in the past

brooch jewellery used to fasten clothing together. This was important in the days before zips and buttons.

craftworkers skilled people who are able to make useful or expensive objects

Domesday Book a list of all the people who owned land when William the Conqueror ruled England. It was written in AD1086.

embroidery patterns and pictures made on cloth, using different-coloured sewing thread

hall the large wooden house in which a lord lived. His family and followers lived there, too. The most powerful lords had the grandest halls. The biggest halls belonged to kings.

harp a stringed musical instrument

jacks counting game, using ball and playing pieces

king the ruler of a kingdom. Anglo-Saxon England was split up into a number of kingdoms. Eventually the kings of Wessex became rulers of all England. Wessex was in the south and west of England

lords the most powerful people after the king. They were given land by the king and they would fight for him. They were also called 'thegns'.

merchant a person who travels to buy and sell things

monastery a place where monks and nuns live. They spend their time worshipping God away from the world.

pottery bowls, plates and bottles made from clay, which is heated in an oven to make it hard

settlement a group of houses, where people live together

slave someone who belongs to another person and has no freedom

trade buying and selling things

Vikings people from Denmark and Norway who attacked the British Isles from about AD789. Those who settled in Anglo-Saxon England came mainly from Denmark.

warriors Anglo-Saxons who fought for their lord, or king. They were rewarded with gold and silver and lived with their lord. Some warriors went on to become important lords themselves

Timeline – Romans, Anglo-Saxons and Vikings

Anglo-Saxon Age

100BC	
AD1	
AD100	
AD200	
AD300	
AD400	
AD500	
AD600	
AD700	
AD800	
AD900	
AD1000	

AD400

AD450   Eastern England settled by the Anglo-Saxons

AD500

Kingdoms of Kent and Wessex become powerful

AD600   Rediscovery of how to make glass

Kingdoms of East Anglia, Northumbria and Mercia become more powerful than Kent and Wessex

AD700

AD710   Trading town of Hamwic set up

AD731   Bede writing in Northumbria

AD789   First Viking attacks

AD800

All Anglo-Saxon kingdoms defeated by Vikings, except for Wessex

AD890   King Alfred of Wessex wrote his law book

AD900

Many stone churches built

AD1000

AD1066   Anglo-Saxons defeated by Normans

Index

Numbers in plain type (4) refer to the text. Numbers in italic type (*24*) refer to a caption.